The Mystery of Nature's Laws

Five Striking Stories of People Investigating the Deepest Puzzles of Reality

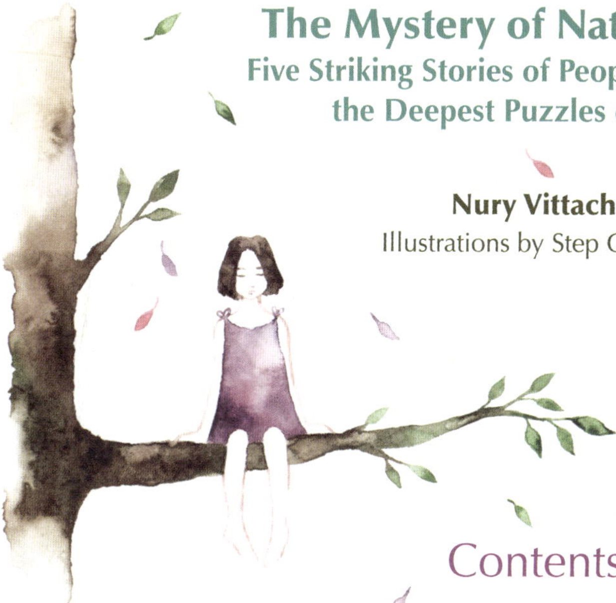

Nury Vittachi

Illustrations by Step Cheung

Contents

STEP C.

THE GIRL WHO SAT AT THE BACK OF THE BOYS-ONLY CLASSROOM

CAN YOU BELIEVE IT? She was banned from university for being a girl.

But they let her sit at the back of lectures and listen.

Amalie Emmy Noether listened and learned, and started writing her own scientific theorems and mathematics formulas.

And would you believe it? They won her a place in history. Albert Einstein, who is often described as one of the smartest people who ever lived, called her "a genius".

And what about the men who worked so hard to keep her out of university? They have all been forgotten!

Miss Noether was born in 1882 in Germany. She liked to be called Emmy.

She was clever and friendly, but had bad eyesight (she wore thick glasses) and spoke with a bit of a lisp (which is when your "s" sounds become like "th", so you might say "toatht" when you want to say "toast").

In those days, girls were expected to do only a bit of studying, limited to music and languages and dancing, and, of course, cooking and cleaning. Only boys were allowed to take long courses in serious subjects such as math, science and engineering.

But when an adult challenged the children to a brain-teaser at a children's party, he was surprised to notice that it was a little girl, Emmy, who solved it much faster than any of the boys.

When Emmy was a teenager, she took exams in French and English and was expected to become a languages teacher. That was allowable for a girl.

But instead, she chose to continue her studies, going to university — despite the fact that universities were strictly for boys only.

The university bosses were not happy. They said that having girls studying "would overthrow all academic order".

Eventually they said she could sit at the back and listen, if she got permission from each lecturer in advance. So she did.

When she finished studying, she got a job as a teacher at a mathematical institute — but because she was a woman, she had to work for no pay. She did that for seven years.

Some people realized how smart she was, and two professors invited her to join a mathematics department at a university. The other professors complained that women should not be professors. One said: "What will our soldiers think when they return to the university and find that they are required to learn at the feet of a woman?"

So she spent four years giving math lectures using the name of one of her male colleagues.

She kept doing what she was good at, and became famous for one particular discovery.

When we study physics at a deep level, we find intriguing symmetries which give rise to laws of conservation, she said. No one had ever noticed that, or proved it scientifically before. "This concept's played a greater part in physics than relativity and quantum theory," said a report in New Scientist magazine.

Thanks to what Emmy and other women proved, girls are welcomed to study math, science, engineering, and all the other technical subjects that used to be for boys only. And you know what? They are not always as good as the boys. Sometimes, as in Emmy's case, they are better!

And if anyone doubts that, tell them about the young woman who even Einstein looked up to.

THE TRUE STORY OF THE PHILOSOPHER'S STONE

FOR MORE THAN 2,000 YEARS, storytellers told tales of wizards and the legend of "the philosopher's stone".

You may have heard of this — in the very first Harry Potter book and movie, junior wizard Harry learns about a 655-year-old "alchemist", a type of wizard, who lives in a forest with the "original" philosopher's stone.

(In some places, the book title was changed to "Harry Potter and the Sorcerer's Stone" because publishers were scared that young people would find the word "philosopher" boring compared to the word "sorcerer".)

But the same magical substance appears in many other books and stories, long before it was used by the writer of the Harry Potter stories, J.K. Rowling.

STEP C.

No one knows who was the original storyteller who came up with the idea of the magical stone which could turn ordinary metal into gold or silver, or bring things to life.

Islamic scholars from the 8th century onwards may have been the first, or among the first, who started to work out how such things might actually be able to happen.

A man in Persia (modern-day Iran) named Jabir ibn Hayyan said that one metal could be "transmuted" into another by rearranging the elements of which it was made.

What substance would make this happen? He didn't know, but he used the Arabic word al-iksir for it. From this term comes the modern word "elixir", which means magic potion — and is another word that we find in the Harry Potter stories, and many other tales about magic, older than those tales.

For most of the past few centuries, scientists were skeptical about any method of changing one element into another, and said that transmutation was impossible.

They said that stories about alchemists, or wizards, were "unscientific".

Then, in 1901, two British scientists were working in a laboratory on radioactive metals. One of them, Frederick Soddy, noticed that one substance, thorium, was changing into another one, radium.

He called out to his partner, Ernest Rutherford. "Rutherford, this is transmutation!"

Rutherford replied: "Don't call it transmutation. They'll have our heads off as alchemists."

Rutherford was worried that other scientists would identify them as would-be wizards and they would be disrespected.

It didn't happen. Rutherford and Soddy became famous. They confirmed that one substance can be changed into another by rearranging their parts, just like Jabir ibn Hayyan had said, hundreds of years earlier.

These days, scientists think the "philosopher's stone" is different for every substance, and better thought of as a process, rather than a thing.

Diamonds are made by the crushing of carbon. Gold is made by the processes that happen in the center of stars.

So next time you read about an alchemist changing one thing into another, just remember that that is one subject on which scientists and wizards have (after many centuries) come to an agreement — the wizards were right!

STEP C
F = ma

THE BULLIED BOY WHO FOUGHT BACK

LITTLE ISAAC WAS BULLIED at school by a boy called Arthur. That's bad enough, but the story gets worse. His mother made him live with the bully's family, so he couldn't get away, but was stuck with him day and night, weekdays and weekends.

Isaac seemed to be a really unlucky boy. His father, a farmer, had died before he was born. His mother left him with relatives when he was three, because she had found a new husband.

You'd think that destiny would give a child with so many disadvantages some good news to balance it out — but this seemed not to be the case. Well, not at first, anyway.

You see, fate also failed to give him much of a personality. Isaac was no good at making friends. At school he sat by himself. Life was miserable.

Now, all this happened in the UK in the 1600s, so a lonely child could not find friends the way modern youngsters do, through the Internet or youth clubs.

So books became Isaac's main friends. He naughtily scratched his name into the sill of the window at the school library as he sat there reading. His favorite books were the Bible and a science book called "The Mysteries of Nature and Art".

The bully, a boy called Arthur, was not just bigger and stronger than Isaac, but he was smart too — he was top of the class.

The lonely boy put up with the bullying for as long as he could, and then he got angry. "Beware the anger of the patient man," he read in his Bible.

Isaac took revenge. First, he grabbed Arthur and slammed his face into the wall. And then he started speaking up at school — and stole Arthur's position as the smartest boy in school.

Soon, Isaac was on a roll. He had an amazing brain, and he seemed to just get smarter and smarter.

Arthur's sister Catherine took a liking to the strange, unfriendly boy — and made a remarkable discovery.

He was not just reading about science. He was doing experiments and making things. In his room she saw a model windmill that really worked, and a device that got its power from Isaac's pet mouse. He had also made a water clock. And he kept huge numbers of notes, in tiny writing, that no one else could read.

Isaac had invented his own language.

Well, you might have guessed who I am talking about. Isaac grew up to become the most famous scientist in history. Even super-brainy people like Einstein were in awe of the discoveries of Sir Isaac Newton.

Being bullied is not nice — but it turned out to be the turning point in one child's life. And if you go to one school in the UK, you can still see a little piece of vandalism by a frustrated child that has now become one of its greatest treasures: the name "Isaac" scratched into the window sill of the school library.

THE TEENAGER WHO SAW THE LIGHT

A TEENAGE BOY WHO LEFT his studies for a break ended up making an important discovery.

When the famous scientist Galileo was just a teenager in Italy, he had to study hard, just like young people have to do today.

One day, when he was about 19, Galileo, who was very religious all his life (even after his famous argument with the Pope!), decided to take a break from his books and go to church to pray.

He arrived there early, and sat in a pew while watching staff get prepared for the service.

He watched the lamplighter arrive to do his job. Today, we use the word "chandelier" to refer to a cluster of electric

lights hanging from the ceiling. But the word really means "lamp of candles", and in Galileo's time, a chandelier was filled with real candles lit with actual flames.

The lamplighter had two long sticks. He used one of them to hold the lamp steady and the other to light a flame on each candle.

The young man noticed that when the lamplighter let go of the chandelier, it swung backwards and forwards. There was nothing strange about that.

But as the lamplighter continued his way down the aisle, lighting the lamps, something curious caught the boy's attention.

The lamps that swung a long distance each way swung slowly. The ones that swung a short distance swung quickly. The ones that swung a medium distance swung at a medium speed.

One of the most important things that scientists do is uncover "the laws of physics". These are the rules that form the foundation of reality, and are of great interest to inventors and anyone who is interested in how reality works.

Galileo wondered if there was a law of physics here, making all the lamps swing the same distance in any given period of time, even though they seemed to be swinging different distances at different speeds.

To find out for sure, the boy needed a clock.

But where would he find one?

The normal ways we find out the time, by looking at phones or wristwatches, were not available to him since this story took place in the 1500s.

He had an idea. He put two fingers on his wrist. He could feel his pulse going throb, throb, throb, throb.

He used this regular beat as a clock to time the swings of the lamps, and found that his observations confirmed his idea: a law of nature operated in the way objects swung from side to side, making them all match.

And so a teenage boy discovered a principle that turned out to be quite important, used all over the world in things such as pendulum clocks.

You're never too young to make a discovery!

WHAT WE LEARN FROM THE STRANGE TALE OF THE HUMAN COMPUTER

ONCE THERE WAS a circus performer who adored his baby girl.

During his working hours, he swung from dangerous trapezes, tamed lions, walked tightropes, and delighted crowds with his magic tricks.

But he couldn't wait for his free time, when he could spend time with his daughter.

When the girl, Shakuntala Devi, was three years old, her father taught her some tricks using cards.

He noticed that she had what seemed like a strange "superpower"— she could memorize numbers and do calculations faster than any adult.

Of course, there were many adults who could do tricks with cards, or remember long numbers, but Shakuntala Devi's powers seemed remarkable. They really seemed super-human. Could it be so?

The circus life was tough. He worked hard but did not earn enough money to pay for school for the child or even enough to buy food for their meals.

Then he had an idea. He decided that the most amazing thing in the circus was actually outside the circus ring, in the humble tent where he lived: his daughter.

So the circus performer left his job and went on tour — charging people fees to see his amazing child do tricks with numbers.

Except they were not tricks. She really could do all sorts of things with her brain. You could make up any impossibly hard calculation, such as "What is 7,928,378,467 times 8,283,739,408?" and she would give you the answer, instantly, apparently without thinking.

She just seemed to know it. And when you checked with a calculator, she was always right!

Her fame spread far and wide. The family moved from their home in India to the UK when she entered her teens, and by the time she was 20, she was on tour in Europe as "the human computer".

Professors in the UK and the US tested the speed of her brain against computers, and she beat them every time.

In one experiment, a professor set her two extremely difficult problems to solve at once. "What is the cube root of 61,629,875?" and "What is the seventh root of 170,859,375?"

Shakuntala Devi gave the right answers to both questions before the professor's wife had even started the timer.

Scientists began to realize that she was not a human computer — she was much faster than any computer.

You'd think that a person with a brain like this would have become a professor herself.

But remember, Shakuntala Devi had barely had any schooling, since her parents could not pay school fees.

And also her personality was a factor. She didn't want to become a professor. She came from a poor background and wanted to use her fame and powers to celebrate her love of humanity.

Shakuntala Devi became a writer of popular books. She wrote one of the first books in Asia arguing that society should be careful not to be hostile to gay people.

She loved the mysteries of mysticism and wrote books about the stars and spirituality, which she felt was a subject that the average person would find interesting and comforting. She also wrote novels and even cookbooks.

In this book, and in this series, we have focused mainly on scientists who discovered things.

But we are including this wonderful woman, who died in 2013, because although she was not a scientist herself, she was important to science.

She established and demonstrated the amazing powers of the human brain — and the over-riding importance of caring for the hopes and concerns of ordinary people.

People are starting to realize that the human brain is not really just a very good computer, but a completely different type of thing altogether. It's an intriguing thought, and shows that whatever new devices scientists and technologists throw up, none of them are ever likely to be as powerful and magical and unique as the human mind.

KEEP READING

READING ABOUT THE LIVES of scientists and other discoverers adds to our store of knowledge, but we hope also leads us towards something much greater, which is wisdom.

This book is part of a series, which we hope you'll enjoy reading, and will spur you on to do your own scientific research.

The creators of this book wish you success in your explorations.

THE YOUNG SCIENTISTS SERIES

Book 1: SECRETS IN THE ROCKS
Five Astounding Tales of People Solving Mysteries Beneath Our Feet

Book 2: FABULOUS PHYSICS
Five Amazing Stories of People Who Solved Nature's Puzzles

Book 3: MAGICAL MATHEMATICS
Five Astonishing Stories of People Who Did Miracles with Numbers

Book 4: BREAKERS OF BARRIERS
Five Stunning Stories of People Demolishing Walls to Make History

Book 5: SCIENTIFIC PIONEERS
Five Incredible Tales of People Who Helped Develop the Scientific Method

Book 6: THE AMAZING QUANTUM
Five Awesome Stories of People Who Made a Revolution in Physics

Book 7: THE SCIENCE OF HUMANITY
Five Fascinating Stories of People Who Helped Us Understand Ourselves

Book 8: WOMEN OF DISCOVERY
Five Super Stories of Fabulous Females Who Made Scientific History

Book 9: THE INVENTOR'S SPARK
Five Marvelous Stories of People Who Helped Shape the Modern World

Book 10: ADVANCES IN ALCHEMY
Five Startling Stories of Chemistry and Biology

Book 11: THE CALL OF THE STARS
Five Wonderful Stories of People Looking to the Heavens

Book 12: MYSTERIES OF NATURE'S LAWS
Five Striking Stories of People Investigating the Deepest Puzzles of Reality

Published by

WS Education, an imprint of
World Scientific Publishing Co. Pte. Ltd.
5 Toh Tuck Link, Singapore 596224
USA office: 27 Warren Street, Suite 401-402, Hackensack, NJ 07601
UK office: 57 Shelton Street, Covent Garden, London WC2H 9HE

National Library Board, Singapore Cataloguing in Publication Data
Name(s): Vittachi, Nury, 1958– | Cheung, Step, illustrator.
Title: Mysteries of nature's laws : five striking stories of people investigating the deepest puzzles of reality / author, Nury Vittachi ; illustrator, Step Cheung.
Other title(s): Young scientists series ; 12.
Description: Singapore : World Scientific Publishing Co Pte Ltd, 2017.
Identifier(s): OCN 969709703 | ISBN 978-981-3221-76-5 (paperback)
Subject(s): LCSH: Physicists--Juvenile literature. | Scientists--Juvenile literature. | Physics--Juvenile literature. | Science--Juvenile literature.
Classification: DDC 530.0922--dc23

British Library Cataloguing-in-Publication Data
A catalogue record for this book is available from the British Library.

All royalties received will be channelled to the National Book Development Council of Singapore (NBDCS) as a gift from the author.

First published 2017
Reprinted 2018

Printed in Singapore